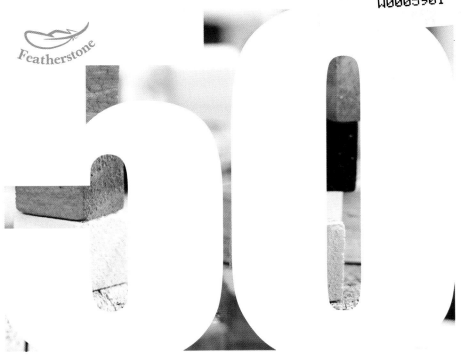

fantastic ideas for
block play

JUDIT HORVATH

Featherstone
An imprint of Bloomsbury Publishing Plc

50 Bedford Square	1385 Broadway
London	New York
WC1B 3DP	NY 10018
UK	USA

www.bloomsbury.com

FEATHERSTONE and the Feather logo are trademarks of Bloomsbury Publishing Plc

First published in Great Britain 2017

Copyright © Judit Horvath, 2017
Photos copyright © Judit Horvath, 2017 / © Shutterstock, 2017

Judit Horvath has asserted her right under the Copyright, Designs and Patents Act, 1988,
to be identified as Author of this work.

Every reasonable effort has been made to trace copyright holders of material reproduced in this book,
but if any have been inadvertently overlooked the publishers would be glad to hear from them.

All rights reserved.
No part of this publication may be reproduced or transmitted in any form or by any means, electronic or
mechanical, including photocopying, recording, or any information storage or retrieval system, without
prior permission in writing from the publishers.

No responsibility for loss caused to any individual or organization acting on or refraining from action as a
result of the material in this publication can be accepted by Bloomsbury or the author.

A catalogue record for this book is available from the British Library.

ISBN
PB: 978-1-4729-4496-2
ePDF: 978-1-4729-4497-9

2 4 6 8 10 9 7 5 3 1

Printed and bound in India by Replika Press Pvt. Ltd.

This book is produced using paper that is made from wood grown in managed, sustainable forests.
It is natural, renewable and recyclable. The logging and manufacturing processes conform to the
environmental regulations of the country of origin.

To find out more about our authors and books visit www.bloomsbury.com. Here you will find extracts,
author interviews, details of forthcoming events and the option to sign up for our newsletters.

Contents

Introduction 4

Plastic blocks

Block rainbow 6
Measuring in blocks 7
Shape fill-in with blocks 8
Building to match drawings 9
Building letters 10
Car printing 11
Blocks puzzle 12
Playdough prints 14
Blocks counting 15
Creating patterns – maze 16
Stability 17
Block biscuit-making 18
Creating story characters 20
Hide a block – guessing game 21
Colour hunt 22
Making useful objects 24
Marble run 25

Classic wooden building blocks

Mirror blocks 26
Stacking tower competition 27
Digital panorama 28
Block tower 29
Block bowling 30
Sticky blocks 32
Famous landmarks 33
Floor puzzle with blocks 34

Construction site play 35
Cheeky concrete 36
Forest trail 38
Drawing around the blocks 39
All things good 40
Ostacle course 41
Build your way home 42

Building with unusual accessories and from unusual materials

Clay bocks 44
Metal can building 45
Chalkboard blocks 46
The block garden 47
In the space 48
Water blocks 50
Cork building blocks 51
Paper building blocks 52
Food structures 54
Cup and card stacks 55
Pebble blocks balance 56
Sponge blocks 57
Nature blocks 58
Matchbox city 59
Tape-road town 60
Edible (vegetable) blocks 62
Block puppets 63
Texture blocks 64

Introduction

The aims of this book

Block play has long been an important part of early years education due to its versatile, flexible nature. Children learn many important concepts through block play. It enhances creativity and provides an excellent opportunity for social and physical development. Classically, blocks are particularly beneficial when children are allowed to freely explore and manipulate them in a variety of engaging ways. The characteristics of block play differ in different age groups, from learning how to hold onto blocks and exploring their appearance, to beginning to transport them and engaging in various levels of construction-type play. Block play naturally gives rise to a variety of activities when children pretend through play: children section off enclosures that resemble gardens, roads, houses or forests. Through building children learn concepts such as counting, sorting, ordering, one-to-one correspondence, size and shape. Through using props and accessories from their immediate environment, children's block play gradually becomes experienced, well-adjusted, practical, socially coordinated and organized, elevated thus to a complex, higher-level, problem-solving activity.

This collection of 50 Fantastic Ideas for Block Play describes a range of activities to encourage practitioners and children alike to think outside the box, transforming 'routine' block play into an enhanced learning experience. The book aims to provide practitioners with a bank of ideas, from old favourites to the less familiar, to use and adapt in their own settings. Children and their play are unique and complex, therefore often difficult to comprehend. For practitioners, it is important to know the children deeply, to flow with their currents, and to extend their nascent theories about how the world works. As they do not readily engage the adults' conversations in order to explain the reasons for their actions as they explore the world that surrounds them, observation is key to understanding and supporting each child on the way they need it. The 'Observation questions' section provides ideas for the adults about how to look at children's play in order to understand their motives, actions and reactions.

The emphasis throughout is on using regular blocks in unexpected ways, or using unexpected objects as blocks for building. The activities are designed to stimulate cooperation between children and adults: children are invited to help in preparation, while adults are encouraged to participate in play.

Handling tools and materials

Some of the activities need an adult to take over if they are to be completed safely. For example, anything that involves handling hot items or substances, or cutting out using sharp knives. Practitioners will know which tasks can be safely accomplished by which of their children, and all settings will have health and safety procedures in place which should cover everything suggested in this book. Some activities suggest places where children might be taken. Readers will know their own areas and the locations that are suitable, and will also understand the requirement for the permission of parents or carers for children to take part in any outings. Some activities involve working with mud, sand, stones twigs and sticks. Practitioners should train children not to put their fingers in their mouths, to wash their hands after using natural materials, and to never use these things to hurt or endanger others. Real tools (small hammers, screwdrivers, saws, pliers and safe knives) that are required in some of the activities are fascinating for young children but practitioners should spend time explaining the risks to children and training them in their safe use.

Block play, multiplied

Block play stimulates learning in all domains of development: intellectual, physical, social, emotional and communicative. However, when a large variety of additional resources is offered alongside supportive adults who engage in active inquiry and creative exploration, block play can enable children to acquire deep knowledge and understanding. When children's actions are explained while they are playing and then built on in future activities, children feel appreciated; their communication skills, their receptive and expressive language and their emotional intelligence develops as a result. When children are asked open-ended questions, their thought processes expand rapidly. While the lessons learned in block play are fundamental to the growth and development of children, when further enhanced by the involvement of supportive adults and the addition of resources and props, block play becomes one of the richest and most complex of learning activities.

The structure of the book

The content is divided into three sections, one including ideas for plastic building blocks (such as 'Colour hunt' or 'Block biscuit-making'); one detailing wooden block activities (like 'Mirror blocks' or 'Block bowling'); and one offering unusual props or block materials (such as 'Edible vegetable blocks'. The pages are all organised in the same way. Before you start any activity, read through everything on the page so you are familiar with the whole activity and what you might need to plan in advance.

What you need lists the resources required for the activity. These are likely to be readily available in most settings or can be bought/made easily.

What to do tells you step-by-step what you need to do to compete the activity.

Observation questions prompt the practitioner to evaluate how the children are engaging with one another and the activity itself, with links to the EYFS Statutory Framework.

The **Health & Safety** tips are often obvious, but safety can't be overstressed. In many cases there are no specific hazards involved in completing the activity, and your usual health and safety measures should be enough. In others there are particular issues to be noted and addressed.

Taking it forward gives ideas for additional activities on the same theme, or for developing the activity further. These will be particularly useful for things that have gone especially well or where children show a real interest. In many cases they use the same resources, and in every case they have been designed to extend learning and broaden the children's experiences.

Finally, **What's in it for the children?** tells you (and others) briefly how the suggested activities contribute to learning.

Block rainbow

What you need:
- Images of rainbows
- A set of plastic building blocks in a variety of colours
- Markers and drawing paper

What to do:
1. Discuss the notion and characteristics of rainbows with children. Show them some images of rainbows.
2. When working with younger children, draw a rainbow on a large sheet of drawing paper to use as a visual guide.
3. When working with older children, let them draw the rainbow.
4. Children sort the blocks by colour.
5. Children create the block rainbow by placing blocks of the matching colour on each colour arc of the rainbow on the piece of paper.

What's in it for the children?
Children will enjoy each other's company and the construction activity whilst gaining basic mathematical and spatial knowledge (size, shape, pattern); learning about colours (pairing the visual colour with the name of the colour) and directions (right, left, on top, around). They will extend their vocabulary by talking as they play.

Taking it forward
- Children can compete against each other when building their rainbows.
- Children can build a standing, raised 3D block rainbow.

Observation questions
- Do the children know some colours?
- Can the children recognise similarity and difference based on characteristics?

50 fantastic ideas for block play

Measuring with blocks

What you need:
- A set of plastic building blocks
- Markers and drawing paper
- Ruler or measuring tape
- Objects to measure

What's in it for the children?
Children will gain a basic numeral and mathematical awareness. Through the connection to real-life objects and a real-life purpose, children will develop an interest in maths and a better understanding of mathematical activities.

Taking it forward
- Count the blocks into sets of five and ten, to encourage children to count in multiples of each.
- Build the block number tower horizontally and use it as a number line to count along with a counting stick or finger.
- Pick two blocks at random and put them next to each other to become a double-digit number; read it, or add together the totals on the blocks' faces, counting the dots.

Observation questions
- Can the children count by rote?
- Can the children use their existing knowledge to guess/estimate?

What to do:
1. Discuss specific characteristics of objects with children (e.g. length, width, etc.).
2. When working with younger children, draw an outline of the objects they want to measure on a large sheet of drawing paper to use as a visual guide.
3. If working with older children, let the children draw the outline or simply measure the object itself.
4. Find about 20 blocks in various colours and write the numerals from 1-20 on one side, using a permanent marker. On the opposing face of each one, draw the corresponding number of dots so that they could be counted to match the correct number. Then lay them out on the floor with the numbers showing and encourage the children to try to set them into a tall tower in the right order.
5. To use it as a measuring tool, lay or stand the tower next to each object, then break off the cubes that are not needed and count how many are left.
6. Try to guess the number of blocks in advance.

50 fantastic ideas for block play

Shape fill-in with blocks

What you need:
- A set of plastic building blocks (large and small)
- Duct tape

What to do:
1. Discuss the characteristics of different basic shapes with children.
2. Use duct tape to make basic shape outlines such as square, rectangle, triangle on the floor.
3. Make the shape outlines larger or smaller, depending on the availability of time and building blocks.
4. Encourage the children to fill the shapes with blocks.
5. Create more elaborate shapes for children to fill in by putting together various shapes, such as a triangle on each side of a square.
6. For smaller children, draw shapes on paper and work with large building blocks only.

What's in it for the children?
Children will learn the characteristics of shapes, mathematical language and the notion of space. They will experience the mathematical rules in a playful way, whilst having fun and engaging in meaningful conversations.

Taking it forward
- Create a challenge by dividing the children into groups and instructing them to work with one colour only.
- Draw outlines of the children lying down as a fill-in basis.

Observation questions
- Can the children pay attention to smaller details?
- Can the children work together, sharing resources?

Building to match drawings

What you need:
- Outline drawings of simple buildings
- A set of plastic building blocks
- Paper and pen

What to do:
1. Look at photographs and images of buildings with the children and discuss the different shapes that buildings take.
2. Ask groups of children to choose a building; then draw a large outline of each building and encourage children to copy this outline to make their own.
3. Younger children can lay the building flat on the table (2D), whilst older children can build upwards (3D).

What's in it for the children?
Children will learn about famous buildings, history and geography, whilst also gaining basic skills such as planning, creative thinking, hand-eye coordination and attention to detail.

Taking it forward
- Set a simple timed competition.
- Make larger group projects that last for several days, for example, 'make a town'.
- Add other resources such as wooden blocks, straws, etc.

Observation questions
- Can the children link different types of information (such as information from the images) and follow verbal instructions?
- Do the children show interest in the world around them?

50 fantastic ideas for block play

Building letters

What you need:
- A set of plastic building blocks
- Paper and pen

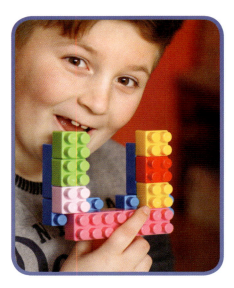

What to do:
1. Discuss the different shapes of different letters in a word. Start with some simple words, such as 'green', 'hot', etc.
2. Find the letters in a variety of media (e.g. wood, playdough).
3. Enlarge the outline of the letters and encourage children to build letters out of plastic building blocks.
4. Make the letters in various colours, then put words together.

What's in it for the children?
The activity will bring volume to the letters as children can take them in hand. They can think out what letters look like, and then try to come up with an answer, which will in turn strengthen their knowledge and their ability to recognise letters in books.

Taking it forward
- Divide the children into groups and aid them in building the whole alphabet.
- Make children's names out of plastic building blocks.

Observation questions
- Can the children notice patterns when studying/creating letters?
- Can the children link the image of letters in various media?

Car printing

What you need:
- Paper
- Painting pads
- Paint
- A selection of plastic building blocks in various shapes and sizes

What to do:
1. Prepare all resources and sit the children around a paper-covered table.
2. Press the plastic blocks into the paint pad and then onto the paper.
3. Try out the different surfaces of each block – the top with its raised dots, the bottom with its lines and open circles, each side making a different and interesting print.
4. Try out different-sized and shaped blocks, and plastic vehicles from building block sets (turning the cars on their sides can make interesting prints of the wheel patterns).

What's in it for the children?
Children will engage in a creative activity, whilst also learning about the importance of making marks. The notion of print will be visible and tangible for the children, helping them in the understanding of books and various artistic images.

Taking it forward
- Work with regular, small plastic building blocks.
- Print in a variety of media, such as clay, salt dough, etc.

Observation questions
- Are the children interested in making their own marks?
- Do the children notice the characteristics of various marks?

Block puzzles

What you need:

- Plastic building blocks
- **Small images** (about 5 x 5 cm), at least 10 pictures
- Double-sided tape or glue stick
- Craft knife
- Scissors

What to do:

1. Ask the children to build 10 small constructions/buildings, each with a flat side that is big enough to place the pictures on.
2. Once ready, stick the pictures on the side of the construction.
3. With craft knife carefully cut the pictures along the lines where the blocks touch, so to create puzzle pieces.
4. Working with older children, cut the pictures in advance of sticking them to the blocks. To make it easier, use only one-size blocks.
5. Mix up the blocks and try to match the pieces of each puzzle.

50 fantastic ideas for block play

What's in it for the children?

When completing even the simplest puzzle, this task sets the children an obvious goal to achieve. They must think and develop strategies on how to approach reaching their aim. This process involves problem solving, reasoning skills and developing solutions which can later be transferred to their personal/adult life.

Taking it forward

- Use the children's drawings to make the puzzles.
- Use only black and white images to make the challenge harder.

Observation questions

- Do the children show simple problem-solving skills such as thinking in steps?
- Can they focus until a task is completed?

50 fantastic ideas for block play

Playdough prints

What you need:
- Playdough
- Rolling pin
- A selection of plastic building blocks in various shapes and sizes
- Plastic knife

What to do:
1. Give each child a small ball of playdough to roll out evenly.
2. Make playdough plastic block prints by pressing the plastic blocks into the playdough; use a small knife to make the edges straight.
3. Talk about how some blocks are thick and some are thin, and some are long and others are short.
4. Talk about the colours and the shapes that the children make.
5. Stack playdough block prints to make towers.

What's in it for the children?
Playdough is great for the development and refinement of some basic physical skills, such as fine motor development or hand-eye coordination. When engaged in playing with playdough, children are required to pick up, pinch and grasp pieces (some small knobs, pegs or chunky pieces) and move them around, manipulating them into slots, sorting them and fitting them into the correct places. This is a trial and error process which involves a lot of hand-eye coordination, where what children see determines their actions.

Taking it forward
- Work with regular, small plastic building blocks.
- Print in a variety of media, such as clay, saltdough, etc.

Observation questions
- Are the children able to coordinate their own small movements?
- Can the children manipulate their body to complete fine tasks?

50 fantastic ideas for block play

Block counting

What you need:
- A large white card
- A black marker
- A selection of plastic building blocks in various shapes and sizes

What to do:
1. Make a counting graph with a line for every number.
2. Ask the children to place the appropriate number of plastic building blocks on each line.
3. Let the children choose what order they want to do the numbers in.

What's in it for the children?
Children will gain a valuable visual examples of the numerals and their meaning. The practical nature of this activity will help children understand the notion of numbers and how they link to one another.

Taking it forward
- Carry out simple additions using the chart.
- Work with single colours for each number to aid children's knowledge of grouping.

Observation questions
- Can children notice the sequence of the numbers?
- Do the children show interest in the numbers/numerals?

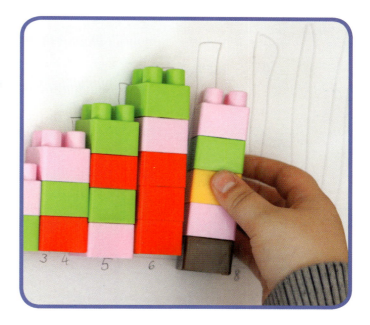

50 fantastic ideas for block play

Creating patterns - maze

What you need:
- Images of mazes
- Plastic building blocks
- Wide straws
- Small cotton wool balls or decor pompoms
- Empty toilet roll tubes or milk bottles

What to do:
1. Explain what a maze is and show the children some pictorial examples.
2. Ask the children to plan and draw a maze.
3. Using the blocks, make a simple maze/racetrack shape.
4. For older children, make it more fun by creating dead ends or a large spiral.
5. Add some archways to make it a bit trickier. Use empty toilet roll tubes as tunnels or cut holes through things like milk bottles to use as obstacles.
6. Give each child their own straw and encourage the children to take turns to blow the ball or pompom around the maze with their straws.

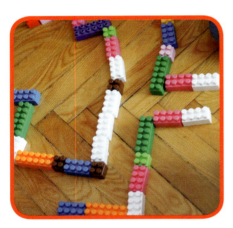

What's in it for the children?
Children will experience building with blocks for a different purpose. Creating their own game will help the children to work as a team, to engage and to solve problems.

Taking it forward
- Use a kitchen timer to set and beat 'best scores' for time without knocking over any blocks.
- Make a maze from regular plastic building blocks on a base plate.

Observation questions
- Can the children think ahead and use basic planning skills?
- Do the children use their own skills to support a group project? Can they share?

50 fantastic ideas for block play

Stability

What you need:
- Plastic building blocks
- **A selection of balls** (big and small; light and heavy)

What to do:
1. Ask the children to plan and build a variety of towers out of plastic building blocks.
2. Set the towers on the floor, leaving a large gap between them.
3. Roll, drop and throw different balls at the buildings to test their stability.
4. Discuss the experience and ask the children to rethink the structures and consider how to design stronger ones.
5. Repeat the experiment.

What's in it for the children?
Carrying out scientific experiments has a lot of benefits for the children, including learning to use equipment safely and correctly; encouraging discussion; observing changes (children have the opportunity to develop their observational skills and identify changes and differences); exploring the man-made environment; considering concepts; exploring cause and effect through various materials; and developing an inquisitive mind.

Taking it forward
- Use different types of blocks, such as wooden blocks, to learn more about the concept of stability.
- Add a variety of media (e.g. paper towel rolls, sponge pieces, metal rings, etc.) to experience what strengthens or weakens the buildings.

Observation questions
- Do the children communicate their ideas?
- Are the children interested in the result of experiments?

Block biscuit-making

What you need:

- Biscuit ingredients:
  - 300 g flour
  - 200 g butter
  - 100 g sugar
  - zest of one lemon
  - 1 tsp. vanilla extract
  - 2 egg yolks
- A rolling pin
- Plastic building blocks in various shapes
- Oven preheated to 200°C

What to do:

1. Make the biscuit dough by quickly combining all ingredients in a large bowl.
2. Rest the dough in the fridge for an hour or so.
3. On a floured surface roll out the chilled dough to roughly 1 cm thickness.
4. Dip the plastic building blocks into flour and then use to cut out the biscuits from the dough. Wash the plastic building blocks thoroughly, then use them as biscuits cutters to create unique shapes.
5. Bake on a lined baking tray in an oven preheated to 200°C.

50 fantastic ideas for block play

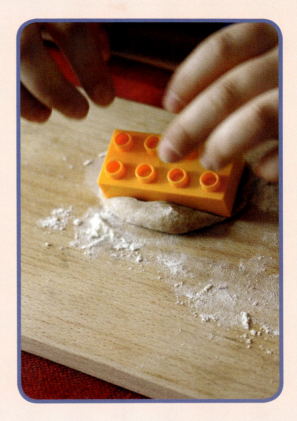

What's in it for the children?

When joining in cooking activities, children gain valuable experiences about taking care of themselves and others. They have an opportunity to participate in processes from start to finish, and to enjoy the fruit of their own labour, which in turn teaches them about responsibility.

Taking it forward

- Build building block biscuit towers.
- Organise a building block biscuits coffee morning for charity.

Observation questions

- Do the children act responsibly when in charge of duties?
- Do the children enjoy working together?

50 fantastic ideas for block play

Creating story characters

What you need:
- A selection of story books (for inspiration)
- Plastic building blocks

What to do:
1. Discuss the children's favourite stories and story characters.
2. Ask the children to create drawings of their characters and plan how they might build and personalise the characters out of plastic building blocks.
3. Ask the children to create known story characters (working in small groups).
4. Discuss 'what makes a person special', detailing the characteristics of each of the story figures created by the children.

What's in it for the children?

Just like in 'real' life, children might love or hate different characters in the story for various reasons (e.g. seeing themselves in them or having similar problems). Because of this natural empathy with the characters, children's brains process stories differently from the way they handle factual information. As their brains do not always recognise the difference between an imagined situation and a real one, so the characters become 'alive' to them. What they say and do is therefore more meaningful. This is why the words and structures that relate to a story's events, descriptions and conversations are processed in a deeper way.

Taking it forward
- Build all of the characters of a chosen story and act it out.
- Organise an exhibition of the children's work.

Observation questions
- Do the children personalise the characters, showing their own thoughts and creativity?
- Can the children link the activity to their previous knowledge of stories?

Hide a block - guessing game

What you need:
- Plastic building blocks in various shapes and colours (some with images on)
- A tray
- A large, dark scarf or blanket

What to do:
1. Put the various plastic building blocks on a tray.
2. Ask the children to look carefully at them for about thirty seconds.
3. Take the tray away and ask them to see if they can describe what was on the tray.
4. For another way of playing the game, cover the blocks after the children have studied them for a while.
5. Take one block away and ask the children to spot what is missing.

What's in it for the children?
Playing this game is a good way of developing children's memory skills and concentration. The activity develops a person's capacity to observe and remember details.

Taking it forward
- Increase the number of blocks once the children get better at the game.
- Place more than one type of plastic building block on the tray to challenge the children's memory.

Observation questions
- Can the children notice small details?
- Can the children focus and pay attention?

Colour hunt

What you need:

- **A colour palette** (various available online)
- **Plastic building blocks**

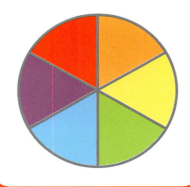

What to do:

1. Print an individual colour palette for each child (or for small groups of children).
2. Try to match the plastic building blocks to the colours of the palette.
3. Ask children to explore the setting to collect objects that match the colours.
4. Assign one colour to each group and encourage children to collect or note as many things in that colour as they can.
5. Finally, decorate areas of the room with particular coloured objects.

50 fantastic ideas for block play

What's in it for the children?

The ability to identify colours is considered a marker and milestone in a child's cognitive process. Early identification of colours helps to create the cognitive link between visual clues and words. In this activity, children can learn colours and recognise them before they understand colour as a concept (basic colours, colour mixing, light and dark etc.). Children can learn that a colourful environment not only plays an important role in the overall aesthetic of a space, it can also impact an individual's mood, emotional well-being, productivity, learning and behaviour.

Taking it forward

- Play sorting games with plastic building blocks.
- Make monochrome images from plastic building blocks.

Observation questions

- Do the children know some colours?
- Can the children recognise similarities and differences when studying objects?

50 fantastic ideas for block play

Making useful objects

What you need:
- Base plates
- Plastic building blocks

What to do:
1. Children can make many useful items out of plastic building blocks, e.g. key holder (fix a small base plate on the wall, place a plastic block on keyrings so as to be able to hang the keys on the base plate); vase; pencil holder.
2. To make a toothbrush cup out of building blocks, build a tight rectangular-shaped outline on a small base plate.
3. Add a row of square blocks on top to make the walls more secure.
4. Continue adding vertical rows until your cup reaches the desired height.
5. Finish with a row of thin blocks for a neat look.

What's in it for the children?
Finding new ways to create items that are useful will strengthen children's thinking skills, boost their creativity, develop their reasoning methods and will also provide them with opportunities to test their ideas.

Taking it forward
- Make items for sale from old, incomplete plastic building block sets and donate to charity.
- Working in groups: ask the children to design and draw items they would like to create.

Observation questions
- Can the children follow instructions?
- Do the children express and utilise their creative thoughts?

50 fantastic ideas for block play

Marble run

What you need:
- A base board
- Plastic building blocks
- Small marbles

What to do:
1. Discuss the notion of maze with the children.
2. Demonstrate how to make a maze. Start by placing a border of bricks around the perimeter of the base board, leaving two openings – this will be the entry and exit points for the marble.
3. Place the blocks on the base board in the formation of the maze, but refrain from pressing them into position until the children are happy with the design.
4. When the run is built, sometimes children place blocks in a way that will not allow a free and smooth run for the marble, therefore it is advised to check whether the marble would run in the pathway before the children start to play with it. This is for the purpose of helping them to understand the notion of the maze and to avoid disappointment.
5. When creating the pathways for the marble, make sure that the plastic building blocks are placed wide enough apart for the marble to roll easily between them.
6. Play with colours: make patterns with two or three alternating colours.
7. Ask the children to create a maze as a group.

What's in it for the children?
Children will gain a lot of valuable experience and social skills through working together as a group. They will learn to negotiate, communicate and share, whilst also practising the vocabulary of colour and learning the basic concepts of direction and pattern.

Taking it forward
- Make individual mazes and organise a timed competition.
- Challenge the children by playing with two marbles.

Observation questions
- Do the children think imaginatively when creating the maze (suggesting ideas, communicating thoughts, asking questions)?
- Are the children happy to share?

Mirror blocks

What you need:
- Classic wooden blocks
- Acrylic/Perspex mirror sheet or silver mirror card
- Double-sided tape
- Scissors

What to do:
1. Choose the blocks with the children that they would like to place mirrors on.
2. Place the blocks on paper, draw around and cut, creating a template.
3. Cut the mirror sheet to the required patterns using the templates – children might need help with this step.
4. Stick the mirrors on the blocks with double sided tape.
5. Encourage the children to build with the blocks.

What's in it for the children?
Building with these blocks creates interesting and unusual reflections, adding an extra dimension to construction and small world play activities. The sensory nature of this activity aids shape recognition and block-building skills, while developing self-awareness, observation skills and focusing ability.

Taking it forward
- Shine torches on the children's buildings to create reflection.
- Observe and draw/copy/photo the reflections on the blocks.

Observation questions
- Can the children observe small details?
- Do the children ask questions?

Stacking tower competition

What you need:
- Wooden blocks
- Sand timer
- Tape measure or folding ruler

What to do:
1. Ask the children to form small groups.
2. Provide each group with equal numbers of wooden blocks.
3. Set the sand timer and ask the children to make as high a straight tower as they can.
4. Measure the finished towers and announce which is the highest.
5. Discuss the details of stability, balance and what makes a sturdy building.

What's in it for the children?
Friendly competition inspires children to do their best. When they compete they will become more inquisitive, solve problems independently, and learn to work with others. They will strive to do more than is required. These abilities prepare children for overcoming problematic situations of all kinds in the future.

Taking it forward
- Challenge children to find block-shaped objects in their immediate environment and build towers of everyday things.
- Observe tower buildings in children's wider environment on an outing; discussing stability, strength and balance.

Observation questions
- Do the children engage in research?
- Do the children try to seek answers when facing a problem?

Digital panorama

What you need:

- **Larger wooden or plastic blocks**
- **Projector or a light source and a cardboard box** (when using this method, one can only project images that are on a transparent sheet)

What to do:

1. Set up the background by projecting a chosen landscape image on the wall. Choose the image with the children, depending on the theme/subject of their play.
2. Set the building table between the wall and the projector, so the children create a second layer of shadow image on the wall.
3. Encourage the children to create a variety of landscapes.

What's in it for the children?

When children make up narratives during their block play without the availability of toy people or animals, they will create their characters using the open-ended, non-representational blocks and construction parts. They use colours and shapes to personalise the features of their imaginary characters.

Taking it forward

- Make interesting shadow shapes using everyday objects to build the landscapes.
- Encourage the children to use their own shadows as characters.

Observation questions

- Can the children follow their own ideas through?
- Do the children demonstrate a simple level of abstract thinking?

Block tower

What you need:
- A set of wooden blocks

What to do:
1. Explain the rules of the block tower game.
2. Build a tower. In Jenga™ the tower is built from 54 blocks, so encourage the children to count whilst constructing.
3. Encourage children to take turns removing one block at a time.
4. Each block removed is then placed on top of the tower, creating a progressively taller structure.
5. The turn ends when the next person to move touches the tower or after ten seconds, whichever occurs first.
6. The game ends when the tower falls, or if any piece falls from the tower other than the piece being knocked out to move to the top. The winner is the last person to successfully remove and place a block.

What's in it for the children?
The game teaches children a variety of facts about balance and connection, counting and numbers, sharing and taking turns and about the concept of time, whilst also encouraging fun and competitive spirit.

Taking it forward
- Organise a DIY block tower tournament.
- Play the game with a variety of cube-shaped objects, such as ice cubes, sugar cubes, etc.

Observation questions
- Can the children take turns?
- Do the children understand basic rules, and are they able to oblige?

Block bowling

What you need:
- Blocks
- Balls of different types/sizes
  (e.g. tennis, soccer, dimple, fitballs)

What to do:
1. Set up the area with no obstacles in the way.
2. Explain the basic rules of bowling.
3. Build a couple of wooden block towers.
4. Try to knock them down with various balls.
5. Discuss the experience, including how it differs when using different balls in terms of weight, controllability, etc.

50 fantastic ideas for block play

What's in it for the children?

When children engage in this activity, they will gain all sorts of knowledge, including facts about stability; vocabulary about directions; physical skills (e.g. managing large movements). While having fun, the children also learn about responsibility through setting up their own game.

Taking it forward

- Make a bowling competition.
- Use cardboard boxes as building blocks to create an outdoor bowling game.

Observation questions

- Do the children use their increasing body control when playing in a group?
- Can the children manipulate their own movements during play?

Sticky blocks

What you need:
- A set of wooden blocks
- Glue or double-sided tape
- Hook and loop fasteners (sheet or tape)
- Sharp scissors

What to do:
1. Split the blocks into two equals piles: one pile for the rough hook sides, and one for the soft loop sides.
2. Cut the hook and loop fasteners into pieces to cover sides of the blocks.
3. Glue the hook and loop fasteners to the chosen side of the blocks, or alternatively use double-sided tape.
4. Encourage children to play with the blocks and create unique shapes that would be impossible to make with regular blocks.
5. Discuss the experience and compare it to playing with plain blocks.

What's in it for the children?
This block play activity requires increased accuracy and a fair amount of dexterity to achieve well-planned, intricate structures. This play is practice in using the smaller muscles of the hand and arm while accomplishing a set of tasks, developing the fine motor skills that are required for future writing.

Taking it forward
- Make elaborate forms (e.g. set children the task of creating a dog).
- Build real-life forms and constructions such as bridges.

Observation questions
- Can the children think creatively and express their creative thoughts?
- Do the children understand the basic physics of various shapes and forms?

Famous landmarks

What you need:
- Images of famous buildings such as the Taj Mahal
- Larger wooden blocks
- Camera, a camera phone, laptop or electronic tablet

What to do:
1. Provide pictures of famous buildings on the electronic device: upload on tablet or take a photo of a book image.
2. Set it next to the children's building area and encourage them to create a similar construction.
3. Tell the children to observe and reproduce the characteristics and landmark features.
4. Take photos of the children's creations so they can copy their own and each other's constructions, using the photos as building guides.

What's in it for the children?
During this activity, children will have opportunities to engage with modern technology and to experience how technology can help people's lives and their tasks. Whilst it stretches their building skills, it also teaches them to pay attention to and to follow directions (other than verbal).

Taking it forward
- Organise an exhibition of the children's buildings.
- Create a book out of children's creations and use it as a building guide book.

Observation questions
- Can the children understand directions from a photograph?
- Do the children pay attention to details?

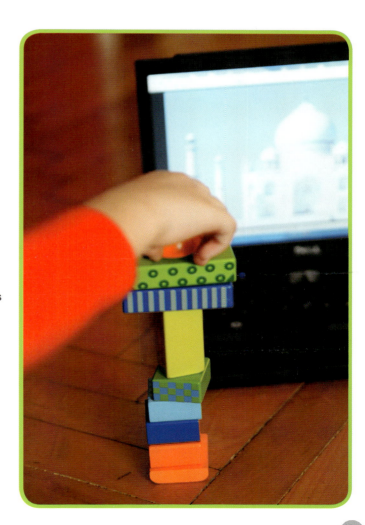

Floor puzzle

What you need:

- **A very large sheet** (or roll of paper)
- **Colouring pencils**
- **A large number of blocks, all similar sizes**
- **Putty-like adhesive**

What to do:

1. Ask the children to draw a large picture as a group. Setting a theme helps to create a cohesive image (e.g. forest, underwater world, etc.).
2. Cut the image into small pieces.
3. Secure the pieces onto blocks with the 'putty'.
4. Encourage the children to put their picture back together.

What's in it for the children?

Learning to recognize and sort shapes is an important part of children's development. Simple jigsaws and other types of puzzles help enhance a child's shape recognition and memory. Children will need to recall the size, colour and shape of various pieces as they work through the puzzle. As children work on a puzzle, they will often develop a strategy to work the puzzle faster and more efficiently. This helps a child learn to achieve small goals as a means toward a larger goal.

Taking it forward

- Make photo puzzles.
- Make individual smaller puzzles from children's drawings to take home.

Observation questions

- Do the children demonstrate increasing memory skills?
- Can the children work in steps and focus until they achieve their aim?

Construction site play

What you need:
- Construction machines (excavator, tractor and trailer, dump truck, etc.)
- Sand
- Earth
- Grey gravel stones
- A large number of blocks, possibly very similar size
- A builder's tray
- Markers and drawing paper

What to do:
1. Create a construction area by dividing the base of the builder's tray into three parts, and covering one part with sand, one with earth and one with gravel.
2. Pile up the wooden blocks on one side of the tray.
3. Introduce the construction vehicles and ask the children to plan and complete the transportation of the blocks. Their discussions should include detail such as: how many blocks a vehicle can transport; what surface can each vehicle travel on; how the blocks can be packed so the greatest number can be transported., etc.
4. Ask the children to document their work plans on their drawings.

What's in it for the children?
Children will gain valuable knowledge about volume measurement in a playful way. They will understand: the basic notion of measurement; ways in which volume can be measured and why this is important, whilst also gaining observational and problem-solving skills.

Taking it forward
- Collect a variety of jars and measure their volume with blocks; discuss how the results differ.
- Guess the volume of various everyday container objects; then measure.

Observation questions
- Do the children have the ability to plan and create?
- Can the children work in a group?

50 fantastic ideas for block play

Cheeky concrete

What you need:

- Shaving foam
- Grey dust food colouring or powder paint
- A variety of spatulas
- A large number of wooden blocks

What to do:

1. Discuss with children how buildings are constructed; watch an informative video about bricklaying.
2. Provide the shaving foam in a large bowl and encourage the children to create a concrete-coloured substance.
3. Ask the children to build with their concrete and blocks.
4. Discuss with children how they have experienced the activity: is it different from the job of the bricklayers? How did the consistency of shaving foam change throughout the play? Did the foam help the blocks to balance or not?

50 fantastic ideas for block play

What's in it for the children?

Simple science experiences will provide children with many opportunities to develop and use important skills such as observing, asking questions, noticing details, drawing conclusions, solving problems, etc. During the discussions of this experiment, children will grow their vocabulary and ability to express themselves.

Taking it forward

- Observe a variety of buildings on a walk.
- Study various binding agents used in different areas of life (e.g. glue, super glue, cement, sticky tape, egg, caramel, etc.) and discuss how they are similar and different.

Observation questions

- Do the children demonstrate a basic spatial understanding?
- Do the children have a basic vocabulary to describe places with specific details?

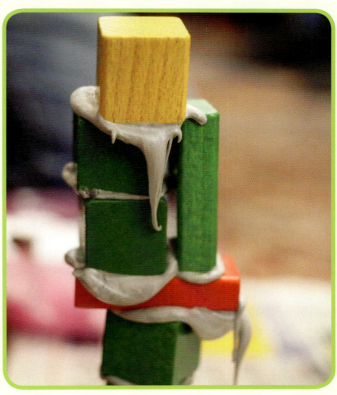

50 fantastic ideas for block play

37

Forest trail

What you need:
- A large number of large wooden blocks
- A large number of small, coloured wooden blocks.
- Paper
- Pencils
- Clipboards

What to do:
1. Take the children into a nearby wooded location and choose a place where the activity could take place. Use an area that is known to the children and agree on its boundaries.
2. Set a starting point.
3. Position the blocks to make two separate trails, a large block trail and a small block trail.
4. Encourage the children to follow the trails in two groups, counting the blocks and noticing things on their way that would make them be able to re-walk the trail.
5. Discuss the experiences of the two groups.

What's in it for the children?
During this activity, children will gain a variety of skills needed for future learning, including how to follow instructions; how to notice and observe small details; how to describe specific characteristics; how to document learning.

Taking it forward
- Ask the children to set the trails for each other.
- Make a map of the area using the children's documentation on the trail.

Observation questions
- Can the children count by rote?
- Do the children pay attention to small details?

50 fantastic ideas for block play

Drawing around the blocks

What you need:
- Paper
- Coloured pencils
- A large variety of wooden blocks

What to do:
1. On a large sheet of sugar paper or card trace several different shapes of blocks, as well as some of the same shape, but in different colours.
2. Ask the children to create drawings incorporating the pre-drawn shapes.
3. As a follow-up, ask the children to draw around the blocks themselves and create a new drawing.
4. Discuss the experience, detailing which drawing was more enjoyable, more difficult, etc.

What's in it for the children?
Learning about shapes, forms and patterns is one of the basic mathematical skills. Children need to be able to understand abstract mathematical rules in the future; this activity offers a playful, individual and meaningful way to gain that basic knowledge.

Taking it forward
- For younger children, use the pre-drawn shapes and the blocks as a matching activity.
- Make a spotting activity by hiding the block shapes in a large/poster drawing and challenge children to find them.

Observation questions
- Do children know some basic shapes?
- Can the children recognise similarities and differences?

50 fantastic ideas for block play

All things good

What you need:

- Wooden blocks
- Food containers
- Colander
- Pipe cleaners
- Straws
- Fabric pieces
- Rope light
- Curtain rings
- Large screws
- Metal lids
- Wire cooling rack
- Paper and scissors

What to do:

1. Discuss with the children what objects they can see and what they find interesting among the household items.
2. Mix the objects with wooden blocks and set children a themed task, such as building a superhero town, making a market scene, creating a forest.
3. Alternatively, read a story and ask the children to visualise it with the provided items and the blocks.
4. Record children's work with a variety of media recorders: take pictures, make a video, write down conversations, etc.
5. Discuss their experiences.

What's in it for the children?

Open-ended, imaginative play opportunities are essential for young children, as when children are role playing and acting out various experiences, they are developing vital life skills. During this activity children are experimenting with decision-making on how to behave and are also practising their social skills.

Taking it forward

- Ask children to each bring an item from home and add them to their block play to further challenge creativity.
- Organise themed block play sessions (e.g. adding only red items; adding paper items; adding kitchen objects, etc.)

Observation questions

- Can children demonstrate creative thinking in a variety of play situations?
- How do children use a variety of objects in their play?

Obstacle course

What you need:
- Toy cars
- A large number of blocks
- Cardboard boxes
- Black marker
- Scissors

What to do:
1. Cut the cardboard boxes into strips; draw a black dashed line in the middle of the strips to achieve a road appearance, and compile a network of roads with them.
2. Use the blocks to create buildings and obstacles (e.g. traffic signs, bridges, steps, traffic accidents, tight pathways, narrow tunnels, etc.).
3. Set a baking sheet on a pile of books to create a ramp.
4. Introduce the toy cars.
5. Encourage the children to play with the scene and discuss the experiences (how problems can be solved and avoided).

What's in it for the children?
Children will learn to solve problems and to approach difficulties with a positive attitude. They will gain a basic understanding of how to look at events and issues from various viewpoints, whilst also experiencing (shared) success and failure.

Taking it forward
- Add a shallow box of marbles to represent mud.

Observation questions
- Do the children think imaginatively?
- Do the children use an expanding vocabulary?

Build your way home

What you need:

- Local maps
- A large number of wooden blocks
- Large card (or drawing paper)
- Pencils

What to do:

1. Discuss where children live and try to locate their address on the map.
2. Make a simple line drawing of the map, adding typical features or places the children like, also adding a sign for the setting and for the children's homes.
3. Provide the children with blocks and ask them to build the way home from nursery/school.
4. Discuss what they travel with and what they observe on their way.
5. Discuss alternative travelling possibilities.

What's in it for the children?

Spatial thinking will be strengthened by learning about maps, which allows children to comprehend and analyze phenomena related to the places and spaces around them and at scales ranging from what they can touch and see in a room through their neighbourhood to a world map or globe. Spatial thinking is one of the most important skills that children can develop as the basis of geography and sciences.

Taking it forward

- Observe interactive maps on the internet.
- Organise a map-making walk in the local area and make a map together.

Observation questions

- Do the children demonstrate a basic spatial understanding?
- Do the children have a basic vocabulary to describe places with specific details?

50 fantastic ideas for block play

Clay blocks

What you need:

- **Clay** (inexpensive polymer clays suitable for baking; or traditional clay)
- Tray or baking sheet
- Oven heated to 120°C
- Oven mitts for safe handling and transferring
- Cooling rack
- Paint

What to do:

1. Start with a soft ball of clay.
2. Roll the clay into a long, snake shape.
3. Cut the snake shape into equal parts. Discard any pieces that are not equal in size.
4. Roll each piece of clay into a ball. Make one ball for each block. The ball does not need to be perfect.
5. Use fingers to shape each ball into a cube. Squeeze the top and bottom, then left and right sides, then front and back sides. Repeat this squeezing process until the piece of clay resembles a perfect cube.
6. Place the completed blocks on a baking sheet. Bake in a low-temperature oven, about 120°C for 15 to 20 minutes, or until properly baked.
7. Allow to cool. The blocks will still seem a little soft while hot; so just leave them to harden on a cooling rack and only touch when they have cooled off completely. Once cooled, they are ready to use.
8. Optionally, paint them.

What's in it for the children?

Through its nature the clay provides children with a sensory experience, whilst also developing physical skills such as strength, hand-eye coordination, fine motor movements and the ability to control strength.

Taking it forward

- Add scent (essential oils) to the clay for a richer experience.
- Add seeds to the clay to achieve textured blocks.

Observation questions

- Can children use fine movements to manipulate materials?
- Can the children link different types of play and use knowledge from previous play situations?

50 fantastic ideas for block play

Metal can building

What you need:
- Empty metal cans
- Strong magnets
- Glue
- **Metal objects** (e.g. tools, cutlery, screws, etc.)

What to do:
1. Clean the metal cans.
2. Glue the magnets inside the empty, clean metal cans and ensure these dry completely.
3. Provide a range of metal and non-metal items together with the cans and encourage the children to experiment.
4. Prompt the children with simple questions and ideas (e.g. Why do certain things stick? How can materials be combined? etc.).

What's in it for the children?
Apart from the obvious benefit of construction activities (including muscle building, developing problem-solving skills, strengthening creativity), this activity offers a great open-ended sensory experience. As children play with magnets, they learn new vocabulary for shapes and characteristics. When children attach and remove magnets from a metal surface, they develop their small hand and finger muscles, essential for learning to draw and to write. Magnets teach cause and effect and other important problem-solving skills that are essential for developing early brain connections. Children will learn concepts such as more and less; on and off; and size and shape.

Taking it forward
- Organise a magnetic tower-building challenge.
- Introduce a variety of pourable things (rice, cornflakes, pasta, flour) to the activity and observe the effect on magnetic power and ability to balance.

Observation questions
- Do the children demonstrate creative thinking?
- Can children construct?

Chalkboard blocks

What you need:

- A large number of simple, natural, old wooden blocks
- Chalkboard paint
- Chalk

What to do:

1. Paint one or two sides of the blocks with chalkboard paint.
2. Some light sanding may be necessary to smooth out any rough spots.
3. Let it set and dry overnight before use.
4. Encourage the children to create special personalised houses, dice, etc. using the chalk.

What's in it for the children?

Chalk is a versatile material for young children; it dissolves readily in water, making it an ideal substance for correcting mistakes. A child can clear their own chalkboard with a water-dampened sponge. Chalk is an open-ended art supply. Children can 'think outside the box' with chalk, drawing with various chalk colours and experimenting with thick and thin chalk sticks. They can explore texture as they see the effect chalk creates on surfaces.

Taking it forward

- Use coloured chalk.
- Purchase or obtain scrap wood or old planks and make the blocks together with the children.

Observation questions

- Are the children happy to use a variety of media to create?
- Can the children personalise their own blocks? Are they happy to work individually or in groups?

50 fantastic ideas for block play

The block garden

What you need:
- A variety of blocks
- A variety of fresh herbs
- Fresh flowers
- Broccoli
- Sand or earth
- Paper
- Coloured pencils

What to do:
1. Section off a corner in the room for a designated block garden.
2. Look at images of a variety of gardens and ask the children to draw sketches of theirs.
3. Encourage the children to build their own garden.
4. Create highs and lows, walls, fences with the blocks.
5. Plant the various herbs in separate sections to create vegetable patches.
6. Take photos and create a book.

What's in it for the children?
Preschoolers and school-age children can refine their gross motor and fine motor skills by building complex structures that require balance, a steady hand, and hand-eye coordination.

Taking it forward
- Add animals and natural materials to create habitats.
- Add dried herbs and drops of essential oil to the play for a stronger sensory experience.

Observation questions
- Are the children receptive when a new resource is introduced?
- Are the children flexible in their play?

In space

What you need:

- A large number of classic blocks
- Aluminium foil
- Green playdough
- Alien- and space-themed books

What to do:

1. For older children, set up the materials and invite them to play with the resources in their own way, whilst recording their play for further discussion.
2. For younger children, wrap some of the blocks in foil in advance and make some simple playdough aliens.
3. Encourage the children to wrap all the blocks and build.
4. Act out alien/space-related scenes; read and follow stories.
5. Discuss how the foil changed the play.

What's in it for the children?

Foil is wonderful for sensory play. It is shiny and reflective, the sound unusual when it is crumpled; it can be scrunched up into a ball and then laid out flat again. In this activity, the act of wrapping helps develop fine motor skills – the children squeezing and twisting the foil to hug the blocks – whilst solving the problem of how to wrap each block tightly and neatly.

Taking it forward
- Add light source to the play.
- Add coloured foil card as a play mat for further reflection effects.

Observation questions
- Are the children interested in basic science?
- How do the children approach new activities? With confidence? With interest?

Water blocks

What you need:
- Water tray
- Foam blocks
- Wooden blocks
- Plastic blocks

What to do:
1. Set up a water tray with water.
2. Provide a variety of blocks made of different materials.
3. Encourage children to build models.
4. As a challenge, ask them to build a tower, a floating house and a submarine.
5. Discuss the experience, including how the water affects the 'behaviour' of the blocks, how different blocks are useful for different purposes, etc.

What's in it for the children?

Children will have an opportunity to learn about basic physics in a simple way. They will see the Archimedes' Principle in real life (how an object in water has two forces acting on it at once, with gravity pulling the object down and buoyancy pushing it up). They can manipulate the objects themselves and experience how the law of nature wins. They will develop observation skills and a wider vocabulary.

Taking it forward
- Add ice-blocks and jelly-blocks to the play.
- Make natural floating and sinking building blocks from wood, stones, etc.

Observation questions
- How do children approach unknown and unfamiliar events/situations?
- Can the children focus and spend a longer period of time on one activity?

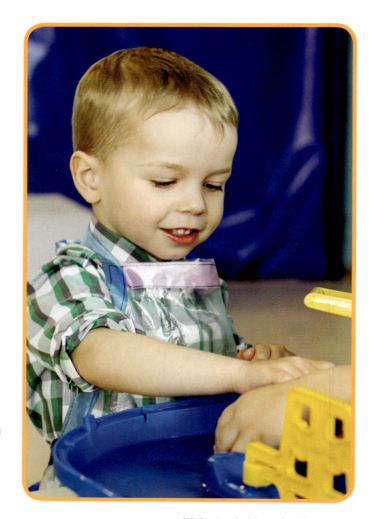

Cork building blocks

What you need:
- Large sheets of cork tiles
- Hot glue gun and hot glue sticks
- Utility knife
- Level
- Hand sander
- Cutting board

What to do:
1. Glue at least four sheets of cork tiles together, one on top of the other to create chunky blocks, easy to handle and build.
2. Once the sheets are set, prepare a cutting surface.
3. Use the width of the level to guide the width of the blocks and trace along the edge with the utility knife (adult only activity).
4. Keep cutting along the line, using a sharp, non-serrated knife to finish cutting.
5. Sand all cut edges.
6. Encourage the children to build with the cork blocks.
7. Add them to regular blocks.

What's in it for the children?
This activity offers children the experience of an unusual texture. Although children respond differently to sensory experiences, the activity can be therapeutic, improve motor skills, raise awareness of how the world works, and contribute to language acquisition. When meeting the cork textures, children loosely follow the steps of the scientific method: they ask questions that describe a phenomena (e.g. Why is this a different texture?); construct a hypothesis (e.g. Maybe it is a different block; or maybe wood?); make a prediction (e.g. If we build it...); test the hypothesis by building with it; and draw conclusions (e.g. It is harder to balance than the other blocks).

Taking it forward
- Use recycled wine bottle corks to create more elaborate buildings.
- Make cardboard blocks using the same method.

Observation questions
- Do the children show an inquisitive nature?
- Can the children work together to solve problems?

50 fantastic ideas for block play

Paper building blocks

What you need:

- Thick coloured paper
- Pens or pencils
- Scissors
- Glue

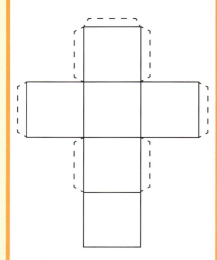

What to do:

1. Using stiff card, make a template like the one to the left (available online).
2. Trace the template onto pieces of coloured card.
3. Score along the lines of the tracing by pressing hard with a pen or pencil.
4. Fold into a cube shape and use the tabs to glue the cube together. Leave to dry completely.
5. Encourage the children to build with the paper cubes.
6. Use different thicknesses of card and paper to create weaker and stronger cubes. Allow the children to investigate the strength of different paper types.

50 fantastic ideas for block play

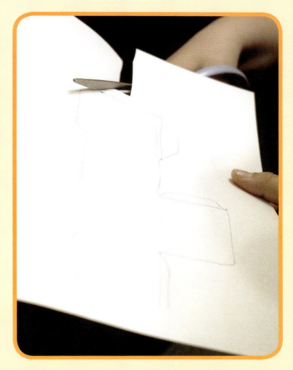
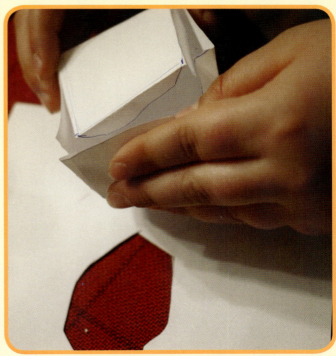

What's in it for the children?

Being allowed to attempt a grown-up task increases their confidence, self-appreciation and self-management. It helps grow their interest and widens their understanding.

Taking it forward

- Make blocks from recycled newspaper for a stylish look and an environmental message.
- Encourage children to experiment with shape and form and create free-form blocks based on their view of shapes.

Observation questions

- Can the children understand safety and self-limitations?
- Do the children act responsibly when instructed to do so?

Food structures

What you need:
- Paper and pencil
- Ruler
- Marshmallows
- Sugar cubes
- Cardboard base
- Liquid glue
- Wooden craft sticks

What's in it for the children?
Planning through sketching stimulates children's imaginations, improves their fine motor skills and exercises their problem-solving strategies. Sketching teaches children to make decisions while improving their visual and perceptual skills.

Taking it forward
- Make these snowy houses as festive decorations.
- Study real architectural drawings and discuss the details.

Observation questions
- Are the children interested in making marks?
- Do children display good memory skills when learning new information?

 Health & Safety
Make sure children do not eat the marshmallows that have come into contact with the glue.

What to do:
1. Show the children some architects' sketches of buildings and ask them to make their own sketch of a building (e.g. house). Encourage them to make these sketches fanciful, as this will stretch their thinking.
2. The sugar cubes will be the building blocks of the base of the house/structure, so start by putting liquid glue on the cardboard base where the children plan to place the house's 'foundation'. This will consist of a first level of cubes. Let this dry well.
3. Keep repeating the gluing and stacking of sugar cubes and marshmallows until reaching a place where children want to put a window or door. When they get there, explain to them that they need to leave a blank space and build (glue) a tower of cubes on either side of this space as high as they would like the window or door to be.
4. Help children to reinforce their structures. Use wooden craft sticks (broken in half if needed) to go over the top of the door or window. Then, glue sugar cubes on top of the craft sticks.
5. Repeat the steps to create more than one room in the house.
6. Take care when moving the structure. Store it for a short period of time only.

54   50 fantastic ideas for block play

Cup and card stacks

What you need:

- Plastic cups
- Pack of cards
- Wooden craft sticks
- Wooden blocks

What to do:

1. Provide a clean, straight surface that children can work on.
2. Demonstrate for the children how they can balance structures on a variety of different bases.
3. Whilst demonstrating, discuss the simple physics of how objects balance, how height can be achieved, how a base is built, etc.
4. Encourage the children to experiment and build freely.
5. Set challenges such as 'build a structure balancing on one wooden cube' or 'build the tallest structure', etc.

What's in it for the children?

Future knowledge and understanding of science requires children to engage with a variety of experiments from a young age. What may seem like simple playing serves as the building blocks for all higher-level learning. This activity offers a tactile, practical way to understand shapes and forms and to see how they relate to one another spatially.

Taking it forward

- Organise a competition for charity.
- Make the challenges harder by introducing limitations, such as 'use a particular hand only'.

Observation questions

- Do the children invent and use personal methods and solutions?
- Can the children focus and concentrate?

Pebble block balance

What you need:
- Collection of different pebbles

What to do:
1. Organise a walk to collect a variety of pebbles and stones.
2. Explain to children that a cairn is a man-made stack of stones, found in different places all over the world, marking special places and used since ancient times.
3. Start by hunting out the perfect pebbles. Flat stones are easier to balance, but opt for a mix of shapes for a challenge. Also collect a variety of colours and sizes.
4. Draw sketches of children's ideas and designs. Make a cairn with a wide base, or build a tall, narrow tower, with one pebble on top of another.

What's in it for the children?
Aside from being fun, making these stone cairns gives children the opportunity to learn about constructing in three dimensions and to consider how to adapt a design to make a cairn stay upright. Children can encounter gravity and practise how to concentrate on a task that requires them to be quiet, to think and focus solely on what they are doing. These are art installations that might inspire others in their natural environment.

Taking it forward
- Berry balancing: make edible cairns using a variety of berries.
- Collect some of the children's favourite objects and balance them on the top of each other so as to experiment with balance in a different way.

Observation questions
- Do children like to be outside?
- Do children express their thoughts and display their skills when making decisions?

Sponge blocks

What you need:

- **Thin washing-up sponges in a variety of colours** (choose plain cellulose sponge without abrasive backing)
- **Craft knife or sharp kitchen knife with a longer blade**

What to do:

1. Decide on the shapes that would make a good selection to build from.
2. Plan how to cut so as to achieve minimal wastage.
3. Mark the lines that will indicate where to cut.
4. Set the blade of the knife and cut on a sturdy surface (adult only activity).
5. Once ready, encourage the children to build.

Health & Safety
Always be vigilant when using sharp objects around children.

What's in it for the children?

Through their textured surfaces, the sponge blocks offer a different experience. The sensory nature of exploration and block play appeals to young children who acquire information via touch. Using multiple senses allows more cognitive connections and associations to be made with a concept. This means it is more easily accessible to children as there are more ways the information can be triggered and retrieved from their cognitive learning centre.

Taking it forward

- Use a variety of plastic and natural sponges for a sensory experience.
- Use the sponge blocks for colour sorting games.

Observation questions

- Are the children interested in making marks?
- Do children display good memory skills when learning new information?

Nature blocks

What you need:
- **Fallen tree branches** (in various thicknesses and appearance)
- A saw
- Sandpaper

What to do:
1. Choose the branches on a walk to the local park.
2. Saw each branch into block-sized pieces. Aim to cut straight, not jagged or curved.
3. Sand the cut edge and the corners of each block, and if the bark is crumbly or distracting, feel free to sand that down as well.
4. Some of the blocks can be additionally cut into halves.
5. Optionally, seal these blocks and varnish, or oil them.
6. Encourage the children to build using the wooden blocks.

What's in it for the children?
Making their own toys will teach children about sustainability. As our population grows and resources become more depleted, finding alternative solutions as provided in nature leads to a more sustainable lifestyle. Guiding children in the same direction through activities will help ensure the planet's sustainability for future generations.

Taking it forward
- Add wild animal figures and act out scenes.
- Add natural foliage, a variety of leaves, and earth for sensory play.

Observation questions
- Can the children think of alternatives?
- Do the children find and communicate their unique ways to play?

Health & Safety
Always be vigilant when using sharp objects around children.

58

50 fantastic ideas for block play

Matchbox city

What you need:
- Empty matchboxes
- Paint or felt tip pens
- Large piece of card
- Glue stick

What to do:
1. Look at pictures of houses in towns.
2. Ask the children to design their own buildings, then communicate their thoughts by discussing and drawing them.
3. Make sure all matchboxes are empty and provide each child with a few.
4. Paint or draw house designs on the matchboxes.
5. If children opted for a larger, more complex building, they should glue the matchboxes together, then paint or draw.
6. Use the house matchbox blocks to build a town.
7. When positioned as required, glue the matchbox houses to a large piece of card.

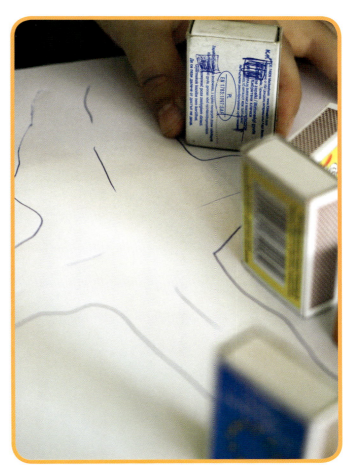

What's in it for the children?
When participating in this activity, children learn to think logically. After a few tries at building a town and watching the matchbox blocks topple over, children will learn that the blocks have to be arranged and placed properly to prevent this from happening. An older child, for example, will also realize that a stronger base can be made if blocks are arranged at the bottom. These logical thinking skills are crucial in a child's intellectual development.

Taking it forward
- Add small matchstick people.

Observation questions
- Do the children approach the activity with interest/manipulate 3D shapes?
- How do the children translate thoughts into words and drawings?

Tape-road town

What you need:

- A variety of blocks
- Local maps
- Images of towns
- Duct tape or masking tape

What to do:

1. Discuss where children live or what they can see on the town images.
2. Make a simple line drawing of a town, adding typical features or places the children like; or simply ask the children to plan a town.
3. Provide the children with duct tape and ask them to create their town's roads with the tape.
4. Provide blocks and ask children to build a town and play with the scene.
5. Discuss with the children what makes a town.

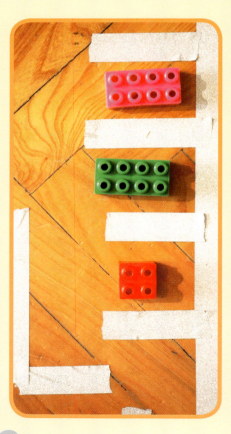

50 fantastic ideas for block play

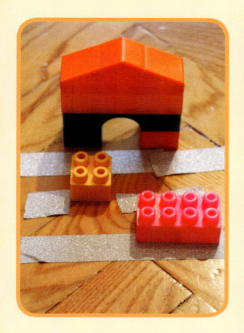
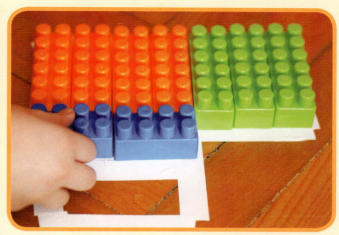

What's in it for the children?

Creating simple maps of familiar places, and then asking children to use these maps in their play is a fun way to teach children basic map skills and develop their spatial skills. This activity will also help them to develop an understanding of direction (which way?), location (where?), and representation (what a road stands for). It will also offer them the opportunity to use prepositions (words that describe an object's location and position relative to other objects, e.g. above, next to, below, behind, and between).

Taking it forward

- Make clay cars for play within the tape-road town.
- Make thematic scenes (e.g. large industrial town, old town, etc.).

Observation questions

- Do the children understand specific spatial vocabulary?
- Do the children create a world imaginatively?

50 fantastic ideas for block play

Edible (vegetable) blocks

What you need:
- **Hard, chunky vegetables** (e.g. carrots, parsnips, swede or potato)
- **Paring knives**
- **Sharp chef's knife**
- **Cutting board**

What to do:
1. Clean the vegetables.
2. Peel about half of the vegetables and leave the other half (this will result in a variety of textures on the finished blocks).
3. To dice, use a sharp chef's knife: trim each vegetable on all sides so it forms a rough rectangle.
4. Next, slice them lengthwise in 1/2-inch or 1.5 cm slices.
5. Stack the slices on top of each other and slice again lengthwise.
6. Cut across the slices, producing medium-sized diced blocks.
7. Encourage the children to build with these blocks.

What's in it for the children?
Children who play games at educational settings involving fruit and vegetables are more likely to develop a taste for their greens; research has found that an early experience of this kind can kick-start a healthier diet later in life. Brightly-coloured fruit and vegetable pieces provide early learners with imaginative play adventures for hours of learning fun!

Taking it forward
- Introduce a till with toy money for pretend market play.
- Make alternative edible blocks from cheese, fruit or bread.

Observation questions
- Can children use tools responsibly?
- Do the children demonstrate abstract thinking?

Health & Safety
Always be vigilant when using sharp knives around children.

Block puppets

What you need:

- **A variety of blocks left from incomplete sets** (wooden or plastic)
- Paint
- Glue
- Paper
- Scissors
- Sandpaper
- PVC glue

What's in it for the children?

Engaging with stories and getting to know the characters gives children the chance to experience a variety of emotions without the risks associated with these emotions in real life. For small children, emotions like wonder, fear or courage can be tested out in their minds as they listen in safety to a story. Young children often experience strong feelings before they are able to communicate them; by discussing and then acting out the feelings of a character in a story, children develop emotional vocabulary and emotional intelligence.

Taking it forward

- Provide fabric and other interesting materials to make unusual puppets.
- Organize a puppet theatre with the block puppets.

Observation questions

- Can children observe the personal characteristics of others?
- How do children tell personal stories?

What to do:

1. Discuss the children's favourite story or song during circle time.
2. Talk about the story characters and their specific features and qualities.
3. Provide the children with art supplies and a small selection of blocks.
4. Personalise the blocks by creating faces that represent the characters.
5. When making wooden block puppets with sandpaper, rough up all of the edges of the wooden blocks. This will help the paint adhere.
6. When gluing on printed images, use a paintbrush to add a thin layer of PVC glue to the block. Then place a printed image on top of the block and gently push it down onto the glue. Finally, add another layer of PVC glue to the image and the block.
7. Build back scenes from the plain blocks and act out the stories.

50 fantastic ideas for block play

Texture blocks

What you need:
- Washing up sponges or ready-made foam cubes
- Sharp scissors with long blades
- Glue
- Natural materials with different textures (e.g. rice, sesame seeds, flour sugar, dried herbs, lentils, etc.)

What to do:
1. Decide on the shapes that children want.
2. Cut the washing up sponges into rough cube shapes.
3. Cut different sizes and do not worry if the cubes are not perfect, as long as they have at least one flat side each.
4. Once the blocks are cut, glue the sides and cover with a variety of textures (e.g. smooth flour on one side, rough rice on the other, coarse sugar on the third, etc.).
5. Encourage the children to build with the blocks and record their thoughts.

Health & Safety
Always be vigilant when using sharp scissors around children.

What's in it for the children?
Children are oriented toward sensory experiences. From birth, children learn about the world by touching, tasting, smelling, seeing, and hearing. Sensory play contributes, as 'food for the brain', in crucial ways to brain development. Stimulating the senses sends signals to children's brains that help to strengthen neural pathways important for all types of learning. As children explore these sensory blocks, they develop their sense of touch, which lays the foundation for learning other skills, such as identifying objects by touch, and using fine-motor muscles.

Taking it forward
- Add to regular building blocks for an unusual result.
- On one side of the blocks add dried, crushed rose petals or loose tea leaves for an added sensory experience.

Observation questions
- Do children engage in a deeper study of their environment?
- Do children use one or a couple of their senses actively when exploring the world?

fantastic ideas for
block play

Block play has long been an important part of early years education due to its versatile and flexible nature. It provides an excellent opportunity for social and physical development by encouraging interaction, coordination and motor skill control. By enhancing children's creativity through free, open-ended activities block play offers a wealth of opportunities for imaginative exploration.

In this handy ideas bank, Judit Horvath provides lots of suggestions for how to turn block play into one of the richest and most complex learning scenarios by engaging children in active inquiry and creative exploration. Going beyond the traditional block activities of building and stacking, this book shows how using free or low-cost additional resources, props and accessories can elevate simple block play into a whole range of higher level problem-solving activities – from block bowling to going on a colour hunt!

ISBN 978-1-4729-4496-2

FEATHERSTONE
AN IMPRINT OF BLOOMSBURY

www.bloomsbury.com